A-Z GUIDE TO AMAZON ADVERTISING

PRACTICAL IN-DEPTH GUIDE

PRABHAT SHAH

CONTENTS

INTRODUCTION TO AMAZON SEARCH ADVERTISING   1

What is it?   1

Why is it important?   2

Are you eligible for Amazon advertising?   5

Getting "retail-ready" for Amazon Search Advertising   5

The Retail Readiness Checklist   5

WHAT FORMS OF ADVERTISING ARE THERE THROUGH AMAZON?   9

Search advertising   9

Sponsored Product Ads (SPAs)   10

SPAs in the search results   10

Sponsored Brands (SB)   11

GETTING TO KNOW SPONSORED PRODUCT AD CAMPAIGNS   13

Automated campaigns   13

Manual Campaigns   14

Keyword targeting   14

Product Targeting   16

Category Targeting   16

HOW TO GET STARTED WITH NON-ENGLISH AMAZON ADVERTISING   18

UNDERSTANDING BIDDING   20

Dynamic bidding   21

Adjusting bids by placement   23

GETTING TO KNOW SPONSORED BRAND CAMPAIGNS (SB)   27

Define your goals & KPIs for Amazon Sponsored Brands   29

What sort of ACoS is generally achieved?   30

Targeting Options   31

A/B testing   34

GETTING TO KNOW PRODUCT DISPLAY ADS (PDAS)   36

SDA targeting explained   37

What sort of ACoS is generally achieved?   38

How to Start with Amazon Advertising   41

TAKING YOUR CAMPAIGNS TO THE NEXT LEVEL   53

How do I optimise my keywords?   53

How do I optimise my ACoS?   55

How do I structure my campaigns for success?   58

Organising your campaigns into portfolios   60

Sponsored Brand Ads (SBAs) and Sponsored Display Ads (SDAs)   61

GETTING STARTED WITH SBAS   62

Key Metrics Explained   73

Managing your Advertising Cost of Sale (ACoS)   74

Advertising Reports   74

SBs Campaign setup checklist   79

GETTING STARTED WITH SPONSORED DISPLAY ADS (SDAS)   80

Key Metrics and Reports   86

SDAs Campaign setup checklist   87

AMAZON ADVERTISING STRATEGIES   89

Useful Tools   93

INTRODUCTION TO AMAZON SEARCH ADVERTISING

What is it?

As the Amazon retail and marketplace platform has developed, it has become one of the foremost search engines for products, with more than half of all product searches starting on Amazon.

Amazon Search Advertising is a paid solution that allows sellers to explore opportunities of getting their product to the top of a shopper's search results. With more and more sellers seeming to open up shop each month, the competition for products to be on the first page of the search results is becoming fierce – making it impossible to scale up quickly without a little investment. If you're just starting out selling on Amazon, Search advertising is a great way to get your product seen and start selling quickly. In other words, with Amazon Search Advertising, you're buying your time.

Amazon Search Advertising attracts a lot of sellers, as its particularly good at driving conversion in comparison to other ad networks like Google. Helping sellers to run profitable campaigns.

In some cases, brands are moving 50 to 60 % of their Google Search ad budgets to Amazon, two media agencies noted. source

Why is it important?

The essence of Amazon Search Advertising is to improve the visibility of your products. Helping your products to sell more, which, in turn, improves product ranking – the amount of products you sell has a direct link to how high up in the search results it will be shown. This virtuous cycle can help you to drive an ever greater sales velocity, giving you quick cash flow.

1. Increase the visibility of the products

Your products appear in a more prominent position at the top of the search results or in another position where buyers are more likely to view your product pages. This can be at the bottom or side of the page, too!

2. Boost sales for all products

Increase sales of your best-selling items and newly launched products with increased exposure.

3. Control seasonal campaigns

Capitalise on seasonal demand for your products with advertising. Tip! If you have products affected by a turn in the weather, you can capitalise on a sudden change, reacting quickly with some new campaigns.

4. Product launch

Every new product takes time to rank organically – it will need impressions, clicks, conversions and reviews. So, to get exposure faster and increase its chance of selling, it's best to use Amazon Advertising.

5. Promote sales

Advertising helps to boost the sales of your discounted products – helping you to reach additional consumers.

6. Improve organic rankings in search results

Although organic ranking and advertising are not correlated, advertising drives traffic to your product page, increasing opportunities for conversion, which is directly related to organic ranking. So, there is an indirect relation. The screenshot below shows a seller doing the best they can to get some initial sales.

	SPEND		SALES	ACoS
)	€7,67	21	€549,78	1,40%
)	€2,27	1	€49,99	4,54%
)	€8,77	5	€159,92	5,48%
)	€39,81	23	€559,72	7,11%
)	€441,73	134	€4.515,63	9,78%
)	€8,71	5	€79,95	10,89%
)	€205,72	48	€1.729,51	11,89%
)	€243,60	39	€1.979,56	12,31%

Are you eligible for Amazon advertising?

Amazon Advertising is available for all products listed on Amazon, whether they're listed through a Seller or Vendor Central account. A Seller Central account is typically for resellers or small brands that list on Amazon as a market-place seller, while a Vendor Central account is typically for brands or manufacturers that sell directly to Amazon. If you sell a product with multiple vendors, only the buy box owner can use search advertising at that time, so, review your buy box percentage and put a system in place to win. Some of the key areas to consider are price, feedback percentage, and Amazon FBA.

Getting "retail-ready" for Amazon Search Advertising

Like a lot of other terms with Amazon, you may have heard you should be "retail-ready" before advertising your product on Amazon. Although this is not a rule of thumb, it definitely helps to increase conversion. So, what is "retail-ready"? Well, it means ensuring your Amazon product page has the best images, best description and customer reviews. Here's a quick checklist:

The Retail Readiness Checklist

I. IMAGES - Product Images play a key role in e-commerce, in general. Having high-quality images showing different angles allows customers to view the product in detail and make an informed purchase decision. Images have started to

surface as image galleries in mobile
search results, as well. So, have
multiple images showing the product,
product in-use, key features and lifestyle shots. The first image needs to
clearly show the product on a white
background, but other images can be
more creative. If you've registered your
products in the brand registry or have a
Vendor Central account, you can add
videos too.

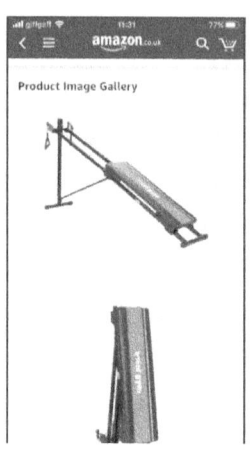

*Tip: You should aim to have a minimum of five images,
but seven is better. Use tools like canva to create enhanced
images with features easily.*

2. REVIEWS - Customer reviews help build credibility and
trust in your product. Having, even just a few, product
reviews or ratings help to increase conversion in general and
it is highly important, especially when you are paying additional for traffic via advertising. Amazon already has
programs like the 'Early Reviewer Program' in Seller Central
and Vine for Vendor Central users to help you build reviews
fast.

*Tip: You should ensure your products maintain at least
a 3.5-star rating to maintain a good click-through and
conversion rate. Always check reviews lower than this to
see if there is something you can make clear about your*

product in the content on the page to avoid customer's
disappointment.

3. CONTENT - Product content that uses the keywords consumers are looking for on Amazon and clearly describes your product not only helps to ensure your listing appears in search results, but will also help shoppers to make more informed purchase decisions. Highlight key, important product features in the bullet points and elaborate further on those features in the description.

　Tip: Use tools like answerthepublic to find out what your customers are asking in Google to help create good quality content.

4. OWN THE BUY BOX - The Buy Box Owner is the seller whose offer is selected for the "Buy Now" button on the product detail page. This buy button typically drives most of the sales for the

product detail page, so you will generate most of your sales while you own the buy box. Whether you are a Seller or Vendor, you'll always be competing against another seller to win the buy box (unless no one else sells on your listing!). As a seller, maintaining the best price, FBA and having good feedback helps to win the buy box. As a vendor, Amazon is the seller on your behalf, so you have more chances of winning buy box irrespective of the price, as by default you are FBA and there is no feedback percentage.

5. ENHANCED CONTENT - Amazon A+ pages are aimed to create a better, more positive customer experience and give shoppers enhanced information about the product. This space allows you to add multiple images, charts and product features. Having A+ pages helps to boost conversion rate, as customers are able to make a more informed purchase decision.

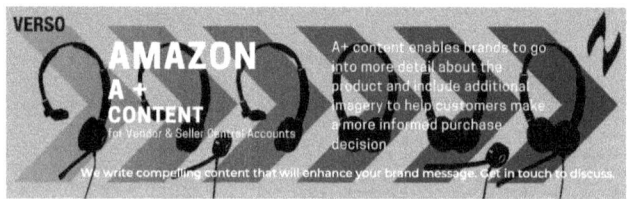

Find out more

Whether you are retail-ready yet or not, you should still advertise to gain initial sales which may be at a higher cost of sales but this will help build product ranking.

WHAT FORMS OF ADVERTISING ARE THERE THROUGH AMAZON?

Amazon Advertising offers solutions across the full marketing funnel, enabling you to build your brand on its platform, reaching a broad range of consumers.

For most sellers on Amazon, search marketing offers a great first step into the world of Amazon Advertising, so this is where we're going to keep the focus of this guide.

Search advertising

Search is a vital step in the digital shopping journey. It's how we make sense of billions of web pages that are online – or millions of products that are on a platform like Amazon. As we've already mentioned, Amazon is now the first port of call for UK consumers when they're looking for a product online. Search ads enable you to ensure your products are visible to consumers that are looking for products like yours.

Sponsored Product Ads (SPAs)

This type of ad is usually the first starting point for an Amazon seller. They're the sponsored ad you see displayed at the top or bottom of a search results page – and you may not realize, but they can also be displayed on a product page.

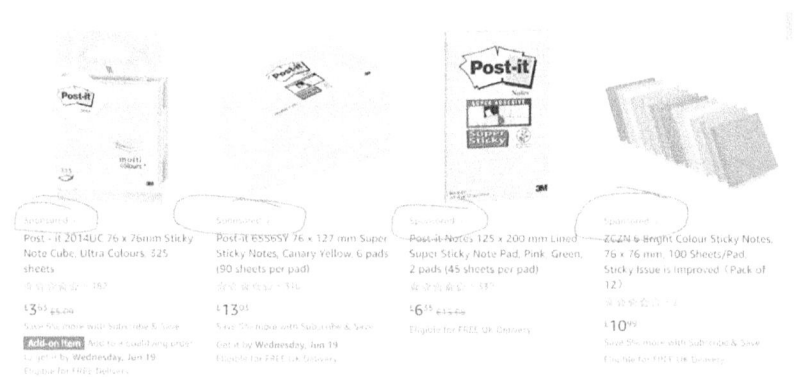

SBA above the search results

SPAs in the search results

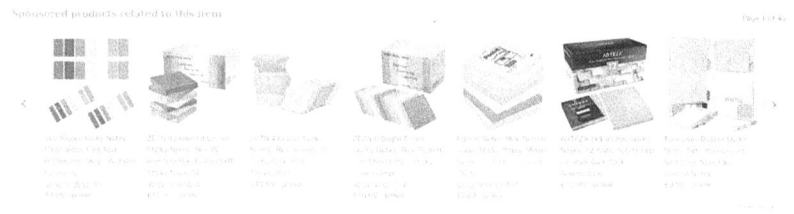

SPAs on a product page

Sponsored Brands (SB)

Formerly known as Headline Search Ads – these ads are displayed above the search results and allow an advertiser with Brand Registry to display three products as well as their brand logo. This makes this ad type great for generating brand awareness and displaying a range of products or generating clicks to a brand store.

Sponsored Display Ads (SDAs)

Formerly known as Product Display Ads, SDAs target other products and categories. You can target your own products to try and cross-sell/upsell, or you can target competitor products to steal away sales, as well as target-related categories.

£15.19
+ FREE delivery
Sold by: DealShaker UK

Add to Basket

Have one to sell?

Sell on Amazon

Save 5%

The Cheeky Panda Luxury
Sustainable Bamboo Toilet...
£26.08   £27.45   prime
Subscribe & Save

Sponsored

SDA underneath the buy box

GETTING TO KNOW SPONSORED PRODUCT AD CAMPAIGNS

Sponsored Product ad campaigns are targeted by keywords, products and categories. Your ads will run only when you win the buy box. If you're running ads and lose the buy box, your advertising stops automatically. There are two ways to run a sponsored products campaign, either automatically or manually.

Automated campaigns

These campaigns don't require any input from you in terms of keywords, functioning like Google Shopping ads. As the name suggests they run automatically, targeting keywords based on the content of your product detail page. Amazon matches a customer's search query with the content in your product title, key features, description, search terms or any other part of your content and displays your product based on relevancy and likelihood of conversion.

Keywords below generated sales because "pigeon baby" was in the product title.

Automated campaigns are a good choice when you're just starting out – helping you to understand search behaviour on Amazon and which keywords your products perform well on. However, it's advisable to cap the campaign budget with, say, a fiver a day to avoid overspending, initially.

Manual Campaigns

These ad campaigns require more input from you, but offer more control to generate a greater return on advertising spend.

Keyword targeting

The keywords you target need to be what buyers are searching for. To help with this, there are three-match types you can use:

1. Broad match: The keyword can appear in similar variants in the search query
2. Phrase match: The keyword only needs to be in the search phrase.
3. Exact match: The keyword must match the search term exactly.

In all three types, misspellings, singular plural and use of conjunctions are included.

The screenshot below gives some examples of how this works, in practice.

Keyword Types Explained

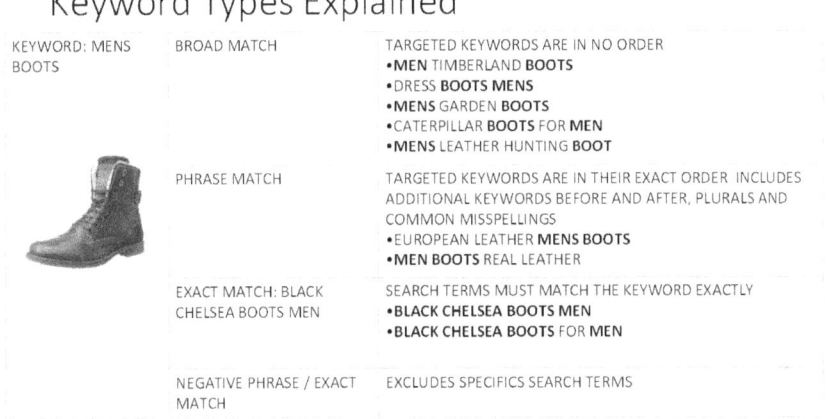

KEYWORD: MENS BOOTS	BROAD MATCH	TARGETED KEYWORDS ARE IN NO ORDER •MEN TIMBERLAND **BOOTS** •DRESS **BOOTS MENS** •**MENS** GARDEN **BOOTS** •CATERPILLAR **BOOTS** FOR **MEN** •**MENS** LEATHER HUNTING **BOOT**
	PHRASE MATCH	TARGETED KEYWORDS ARE IN THEIR EXACT ORDER INCLUDES ADDITIONAL KEYWORDS BEFORE AND AFTER, PLURALS AND COMMON MISSPELLINGS •EUROPEAN LEATHER **MENS BOOTS** •**MEN BOOTS** REAL LEATHER
	EXACT MATCH: BLACK CHELSEA BOOTS MEN	SEARCH TERMS MUST MATCH THE KEYWORD EXACTLY •**BLACK CHELSEA BOOTS MEN** •**BLACK CHELSEA BOOTS** FOR **MEN**
	NEGATIVE PHRASE / EXACT MATCH	EXCLUDES SPECIFICS SEARCH TERMS

Amazon Manual Keywords Match types - the bold words are actual keywords/ customer query.

There's also another type of keyword - Negative keywords. They help you to eliminate wastage. You may want to avoid very generic terms that are likely to be more competitive and, therefore, more expensive. Although, when they're starting out, lots of advertisers like to keep generic terms in so they can start to better understand customer search behaviour.

Like Google, Amazon allows you to see the customer search term via a "search term" report. This allows you to see how each in your campaign is performing against a set of campaign metrics. We'll discuss this later on page 19

Product Targeting

This is new to most advertisers and is geared toward targeting any products on Amazon. Your product is displayed at the bottom of a targeted product detail page under "Sponsored products related to this item", as seen in the picture below.

This enables you to follow three strategies:

1. Attack competitors' products with your best sellers or entry-level products
2. Complement similar products often sold with yours or bought by the same audience
3. Block with your own products by cross-selling or upselling products

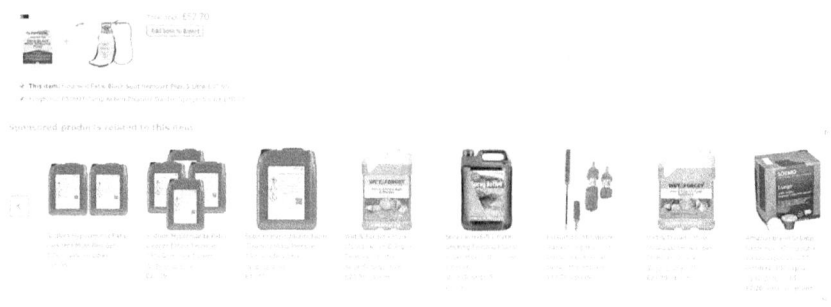

Category Targeting

These are created with product targeted ads and target shoppers in a certain category. Displaying your product at the bottom of the product detail page under "Sponsored products related to this item" as seen in the picture below, allowing you to target:

1. Specific sub-product category
2. Root product category

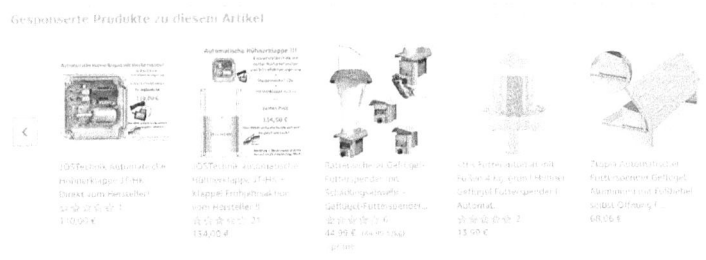

Category Ads result in Amazon.de

Automated targeting	Manual targeting
Keyword targets are based on your title, key features, description and search terms.	You have full control of which keywords are targeted.
Ability to add negative search terms.	
You can also add negative keywords, based on the search term report.	You can also add negative keywords
Can adjust placement bids.	Choose from three keywords match type

HOW TO GET STARTED WITH NON-ENGLISH AMAZON ADVERTISING

Amazon Advertising in other countries like Germany, for instance, works the same way as in the UK or the US. However, not having the language understanding is the biggest barrier when advertising in other marketplaces. That being said, taking some basic steps, you can now advertise and generate effective results. Take a look at these basic steps below:

Product/Category Targeting Ads - Amazon's product and category targeting options give a fantastic opportunity to target products and categories that are similar to yours. As long as you know what other products are similar to yours, the language barrier is not an issue. Another way is to find the similar products as used in the UK. You can do this easily using the same ASINs. Amazon's unique ASIN system is the same globally as long as they use the same EAN/UPCs.

Start with auto ads - As auto ads do not need keyword targets, you can start with this campaign type easily. However, you need to ensure your product content is optimised with the right, relevant keywords. You can then create manual targeted KW campaigns based on the keywords that generated sales in your auto campaigns.

Use Amazon suggestions - Along with targeted campaigns, as mentioned above, Amazon suggestions are good to use as well.

Use automated translation tools - Using sonar keyword research, along with reverse ASIN search, creates a list of keywords and takes advantage of Google translate function to understand the relevancy. This is not perfect, but can help you to get started.

Using these principles, we have worked on Amazon France and seen considerable growth. Check out the case study below:

Amazon UK Advertising - 5:1 ROAS Find out more

UNDERSTANDING BIDDING

Amazon advertising runs ads based on an auction system. Advertisers bidding on a particular keyword, product or category set a maximum bid, and the winner then pays one pence or cent over their rivals. For example, if you're bidding £1.00 per click for a campaign, you agree to pay up to £1.00 but, if your competitor bids £0.75 for their campaign you'll pay £0.76.

Currently, Amazon allocates 50p as a default bid, but it's always worth starting with a lower bid if possible. The worst-case scenario is you gain no impressions, in which case you can always increase your bid, but this stops overspending.

Amazon uses similar concepts as Google to decide relevance. Relevance is a really important concept as it drives which ASINs rank the highest organically for a particular query and allows advertisers to win keyword bids for less money.

Amazon's ranking algorithm considers:

- Sales History
- Impressions
- Click-Through-Rate
- Product Description
- Image Quality
- Reviews
- Keyword Bidding

Hopefully, you'll see from the above list just why your content is so important, which is why your content optimisation should be the foremost priority! We have written a detailed guide on this topic. Get a copy following the link below:

PULSIN

Strategy, Content, A+ & Advertising

Health & Personal Care

Amazon Vendor - 30% increase in YOY COGS Find out more

Dynamic bidding

Recently, Amazon added Amazon Placement Strategy within Sponsored Product Campaigns. This can be seen on the top of the campaign on the placement tab. Here you have three bidding options:

- **Fixed bids:** use the amount you've input all the time
- **Dynamic bids - down only:** reduces your bid when the Amazon system thinks your product is less likely to convert
- **Dynamic bids – up and down:** will also increase up to double your bid if the system thinks you're more likely to convert

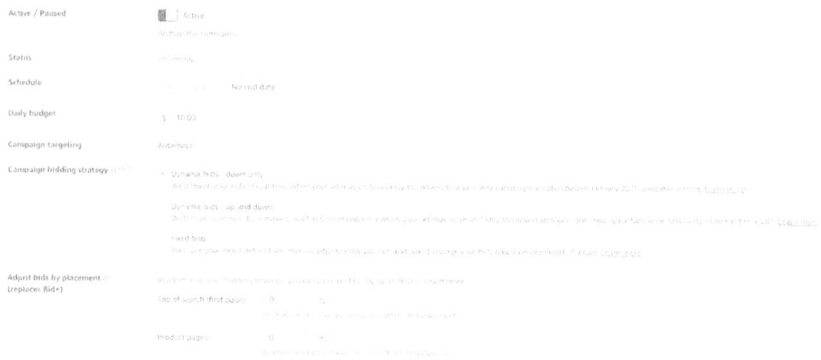

Campaign bidding strategy

Strategy	When to use?
Dynamic bids - down only	Not sure about the level of conversion, for new campaigns
Dynamic bids - up and down	The results are looking good, ACoS is profitable
Fixed bids	You are focused on limited budget spend

Adjusting bids by placement

You can also use the same tab to increase/decrease up to 9x your bid value to target a particular ad placement. This helps you to ensure your product visibility by being displayed at the premium top of search spots on the first page. These are a number of placements where a search ad can be displayed on Amazon.

1. Top of the page

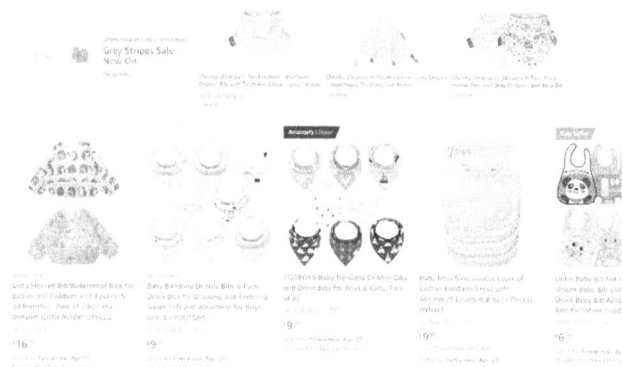

2. Bottom of the page

3. Below Key Features

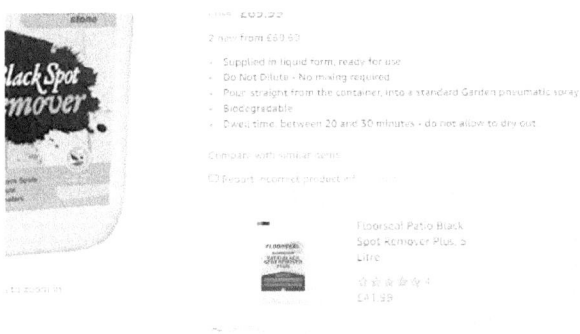

e) In the carousel under the description of the product only if ASIN or category targeted

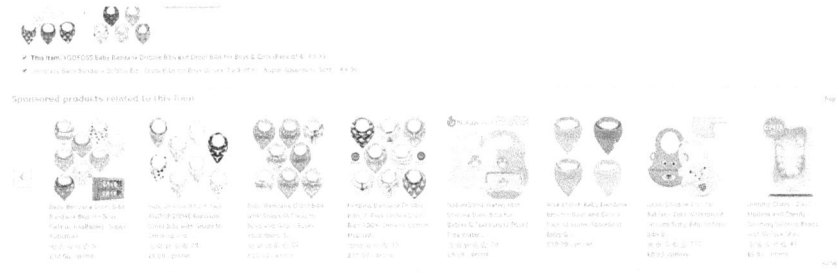

Which bidding strategy would you implement in the two situations below?

Placement	Bidding strategy	Bid adjustment	Impressions	Clicks	CTR	Spend	CPC	Orders	Sales	ACoS
Total			182,434	6,442	3.3%	£1,813.44	£0.22	149	£8,646.76	20.90%
Top of search	Dynamic bidding (down only)		1,672	143	8.55%	£17.91	£0.13	16	£473.96	3.90%
Product detail pages	Dynamic bidding (down only)		176,593	4,427	8.18%	£102.07	£0.23	81	£7,861.19	25.65%
Rest of site	Dynamic bidding (down only)		316,974	2,214	7.47%	£892.43	£0.23	66	£2,786.34	40.70%

Situation 1

Placement	Bidding strategy	Bid adjustment	Impressions	Clicks	CTR	Spend	CPC	Orders	Sales	ACoS
Total			647,476	3,745	0.50%	£853.42	£0.22	23	£4,994.38	17.60%
Top of search	Dynamic bidding (down only)		4,165	103	2.24%	£20.66	£0.16	7	£42.55	48.60%
Product detail pages	Dynamic bidding (down only)		523,993	3,442	0.45%	£289.36	£0.19	21	£1,641.72	14.60%
Rest of site	Dynamic bidding (down only)		18,479	274	0.92%	£96.20	£0.21	1	£159.14	49.20%

Situation 2

FIND OUT MORE

GETTING TO KNOW SPONSORED BRAND CAMPAIGNS (SB)

Sponsored Brand campaigns appear on the topmost part of the Amazon SERP with three of your chosen products as a banner, on the left-hand rail, or at the bottom of the page with your brand logo and a tagline. Recently, they've also started appearing on the product page, just underneath your images and key features.

Another really interesting area of development for SBAs is the recent launch of Video ads. For now, they are only available in the UK & DE, with DE only having been fully rolled out late last month. As an FYI, Amazon recommends video ads of <15s focusing purely on product and features, and bid structures similar to a regular SBA campaign, but the ROAS is a lot higher.

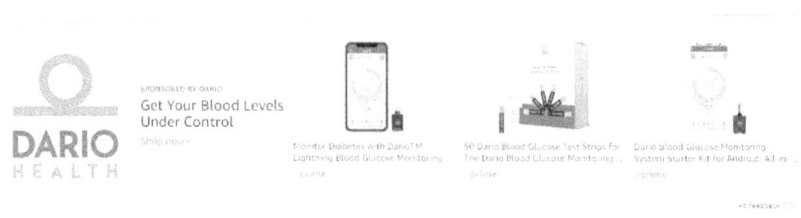

SB campaigns appearing at the top of the search

SB campaigns appearing at the bottom of the search

SB campaigns are a great way to generate brand awareness with target keywords. These ads can either link through to a node page, advertising the three selected products, or your Amazon store. It's available for Vendor Central and Seller Central users with Brand Registry. Once the campaigns are running, you can see keyword performance reports to see which keywords perform better.

SBs are typically less efficient than SPAs, so we would usually recommend implementing them once you have built a decent amount of sales. However, sometimes, it may be a good idea to test SBs alongside SPAs to get generate high visibility of your product or brand.

Define your goals & KPIs for Amazon Sponsored Brands

Drive brand awareness: If this is your aim, take note of impressions to give you a sense of brand awareness.

Drive brand consideration and sales: By linking to a brand store, you're able to bring shoppers to a branded environment where you can present your product range as a whole. This enables you to educate a user on your most premium products and drive a higher average selling price. The brand store performance and sales are reported separately to your campaigns.

Competitive Bidding: If your goal is to appear at the top of the search and above your competitors, then ensure you are bidding competitively. Check your impressions regularly. If your impressions are getting lower, then probably your competitor has taken the space.

Some of the KPIs for SB campaigns are:

New to Brand metrics (NTB): This tells you how many first-time buyers purchased your product through the SBA. The screenshot below shows on average about 90% of sales are new customer acquisition.

Cost per Acquisition (CPA): This is an important metric that allows you to find out the aggregated cost of acquiring a new customer. Calculated by dividing ad spend by a number of orders, CPA can be analysed in campaign structure. The screenshot below shows an average of about £3.00 cost per acquisition.

CPA = Ad Spend / Number of Conversions

Conversion Rate: The Conversion Rate of a campaign is the percentage of people who clicked on an ad and then completed sales. The screenshot below shows about 10% conversion rate.

	A	K	M	O	P	Q	R	S	T	U	V	W
	Campaigns	Clicks	Spend(GB)	Orders	Sales(G)	Conversion Rt	CPA	ACoS(%)	NTB orders	% of orders NT	NTB sales	% of sales NTE
2	Campaign 1	6651	2222	659	11922	10	3.38	18.63	265	91.38	4965.38	92.32
3	Campaign 2	4164	675	385	3610	11	1.76	18.69	171	84.24	1616.47	86.27
4	Campaign 3	3362	652	377	3400	9	1.73	19.17	284	86.06	2661.23	85.84
5	Campaign 4	2659	412	459	2710	6	0.90	15.21	295	93.95	1679.37	93.94
6	Campaign 5	3034	522	238	2514	13	2.19	20.77	76	81.72	790.51	81.94

What sort of ACoS is generally achieved?

By default, we see £1.50 bid per click and generally up to these campaigns are around 4x more expensive than SPAs. For brands with a higher number of SKUs, the higher level of visibility in search driving to a brand store can make SBs worth the comparatively higher costs.

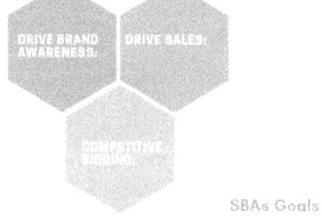

SBAs Goals

It's important to be clear on your advertising goal when you launch SB campaigns. You may want to promote your seasonal products or generate brand visibility for a new range. Based on these goals, we can measure the effectiveness of your campaigns.

We have seen ACoS from 10% upward, but there are new reporting metrics that can help justify the use of SB campaigns. In the screenshot above, the ACoS is probably too high, but it's worth spending the money, as most of the customers are new.

Targeting Options

Targeting

☐ Keyword targeting
Choose keywords to help your products appear in shopper searches. Learn more

Use this strategy when you know the search terms that customers use to search products similar to yours.

☐ Product targeting
Choose specific products, categories, brands, or other product features to target your ads. Learn more

Use this strategy to reach shoppers who browse or search products in a set of categories or brands

SBs can target keywords, categories and products. Below are some tips on keywords targeting:

Converting keywords from SPA: Generally, SB ads are run after you have experimented with SPAs and by this time you'll know which keywords work for you. So, you can focus on the keywords that you know work well, giving more chances of selling.

Brand names: Targeting your own brand name will be cheaper for you to advertise and you can upsell to existing customers, showing them more premium products through your store. If you don't have a well-known brand, search targeting competitors is another strategy to gain visibility and display your alternative. You should also be aware if your brand is popular; the chance of competitors bidding on your brand is pretty high.

Related product keywords: Targeting keywords for products that are complementary or frequently bought-together products is another good strategy to increase visibility.

Like SPA there are three match types: broad, phrase and exact. There isn't grouping available so you can use all three match types at the same time to check the effectiveness of keyword match types.

Although it's not guaranteed, Amazon is known to pay for the Google advertisement for the SB campaigns, where appropriate, as seen on the result below. So, you can gain extra traffic straight from Google search and, because Amazon pages usually have a higher conversion rate compared to your own website, the chance of selling is high.

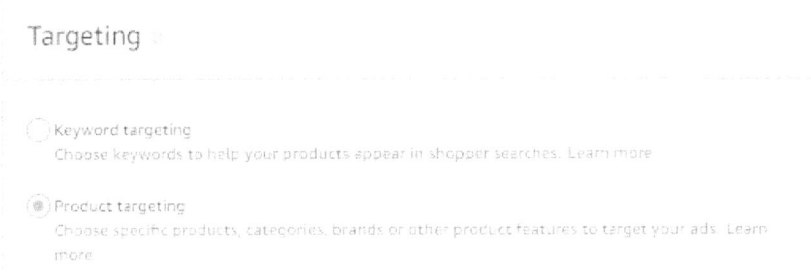

blood glucose test kit

All   Shopping   Images   Videos   News   More

About 60,200,000 results (0.55 seconds)

Diabetes Self Test Kits | Online Diabetes Results
Ad www.letsgetchecked.com/Diabetes/Test ▾ 020 3936 4095
Convenient Home Diabetes Testing. No Need To Visit A Clinic or Take Time Off Work
Online Including Direct Contact To An Experienced Medical Team. Medical Experts &
Accurate Results. Free Delivery. Prescriptions Provided. Accurate CE Marked Tests.
Diabetes Test - from £39.00 - At Home HbA1c Test · More ▾

The FreeStyle Libre System | Blood Glucose Testing
Ad www.freestylelibre.co.uk/ ▾
No Lancets. No Test Strips & No Blood - You Can Do It With The FreeStyle Libre. Ea

Blood Glucose Testing Kits | at Amazon.co.uk
Ad www.amazon.co.uk/shopping ▾
Check Out our Selection & Order Now. Free UK Delivery on Eligible Orders!

Targeting

○ Keyword targeting
    Choose keywords to help your products appear in shopper searches. Learn more

◉ Product targeting
    Choose specific products, categories, brands or other product features to target your ads. Learn
    more

Product targeting: Product targeting allows SBs to target products or categories. This basically works the same as it does with SPAs. Your customers find your product while browsing product detail pages and categories or when searching for products on Amazon.

Category targeting: Again, this works basically the same as it does with SPAs, targeting relevant categories, or you can target refined categories.

Unlike SPAs, product and category targets do not display your product on sponsor-related products areas, but via keywords related to that particular product.

GET IN TOUCH TO BOOK A SESSION

A/B testing

SB allows some level of creativity, including custom headline and image, the order of product display and landing page. So, you can create multiple advertisements and run simultaneously to get the best result.

Brand Logo or Life Style Image

Tagline should entice customer. Consider mobile view as this is where most people shop. Mention USP but avoid promotions and claims like #1 best seller

SPONSORED BY TEST YOUR INTOLERANCE

Get food intolerance test

Shop now

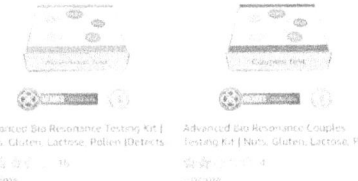

Advertise your Amazon store or create your own landing page

Order the products in the way you'd like customers to see

GETTING TO KNOW PRODUCT DISPLAY ADS (PDAS)

SDAs boost product visibility by targeting specific ASINs. Brands can target similar or complementary products. SDAs are currently available for Vendor Central and are being rolled out across Seller Central in the US and UK, so this may not be available for all sellers yet. SDAs are visible on:

- Product Detail Pages on Desktop and Mobile
- Search Results Pages
- Customer Review Pages
- Top of the Offer Listing Pages

SDAs examples

SDA targeting explained

SDAs are relatively easy to set up and don't require any keyword research. It can be very useful to build product awareness based on interest as well as retargeting high-intent shoppers who viewed specific product ASINs.

Instead of keyword targeting, there are two different types of targeting for SDAs for Amazon Vendors in the UK:

Audience Targeting finds potential customers based on their shopping habits. Selecting categories to display your ads means you can attract shoppers as they browse products that might be ranked higher in search than your own.

You can think of these ads similar to a display ad, targeting shoppers in more of a lifestyle approach. By focusing your tagline on a clear consumer benefit of your product, you can look to drive consideration of your brand; so the next time they are in the market for a product like yours, they'll already know your brand. For this type of goal, you'll want to focus on generating as many clicks as possible.

Currently, SDAs are available to brands in the US Seller Central accounts with only placements across Amazon's third-party display network. Engagement is limited to shoppers who have previously viewed your products or products similar to yours in the last 30 days, excluding shoppers who have purchased a similar product.

Product Targeting allows you to target specific product pages. Here, you can specify products or categories. Amazon limits your category choice based on your product category. It can be powerful because you can display products against your competing or complementary products. Others display against their own products as a defensive marketing tactic to block competitors and upsell through their own range. Whichever target you are using, ensure that your SDAs include your logo and a tagline.

What sort of ACoS is generally achieved?

SDA cost depends on the products you're targeting and the market you are in. If you are in a saturated market, then your cost will be high, whereas niche markets tend to be lower. The screenshot below shows ACoS starting from 6% to 23%.

Start date	Orders	▼ Sales	ACOS
	1,003	£10,299.17	16.29%
7/1/2018	168	£2,124.91	11.88%
7/1/2018	189	£1,705.02	23.53%
28/7/2018	53	£941.79	6.48%

Amazon EU Sales Growth via Advertising Find out more

HOW TO START WITH AMAZON ADVERTISING

We've been through all the different ad types available in Amazon, but how do we actually get started with Amazon Advertising? Advertising on Amazon starts from the very beginning with content optimisation. When buyers land on your product page, you want them to see detailed information about the product and excellent photos. Winning the buy box is a prerequisite of Amazon Advertising. It's a complex mechanism, but the main criteria for winning the buy box is price, fulfillment method and feedback percentage.

Note: If you have problems with one product and start receiving too much negative feedback, you'll lose the buy box.

Create Amazon Sponsored Products campaign

Amazon Advertising screenshot

As a Seller Central user, you can access campaigns via Campaign Manager, the "Advertising" tab, including "Manage Campaigns"> "Create Campaign".

Then simply follow the steps given below.

Step 1

When setting up campaigns, it is beneficial to have a descriptive naming structure. This helps when analysing and also makes it easier for other people viewing the account to understand what campaigns are what.

Step 2

Fix your daily budget. Initially, for all new campaigns, setting a fiver a day budget to limit the spending is recommended. Depending on the success of the campaigns, you can then increase/decrease your budget.

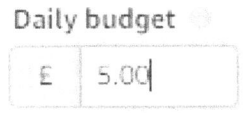

Step 3

Start and End Dates are there to help you decide seasonal campaigns. It's also best to have an end date for all new campaigns, just in case you don't remember to revisit. Please note that this can be detrimental. If the campaign ends and it's been running well, you can lose the history of the campaign. Campaigns can take a little time to hit maturity for what you're targeting.

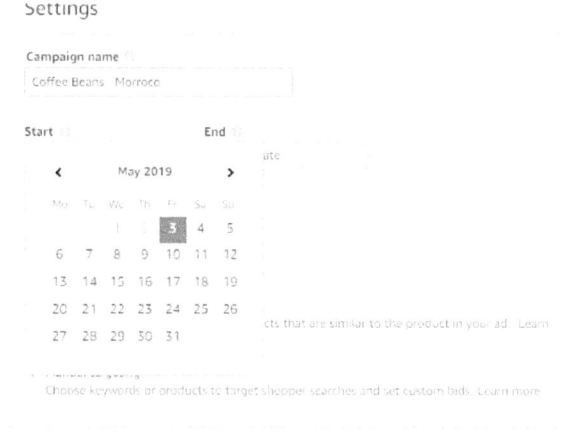

Step 4

Choose between automated and manual

Automated Campaigns: You can use these campaigns when you're using ads for the first time. It allows you to get converting keywords via the search term report. Although you have less control, your budget cap limits how much will be spent.

Manual Campaigns: This works well if you have a list of keywords.

Step 5

Create ad groups with similar products. This allows you to focus on the same keywords for the group.

Step 6

Set the bids for your ad groups. With automated campaigns, you set the bid for the whole group and for the manual you set for a bid for either the group or by individual keywords. Amazon does not recommend bids for the auto campaigns, but does the manual campaigns as seen below.

You're done! Sit back, relax and wait for your results.

Key Metrics Explained

- *Impressions* are the total number of times your ad was seen.
- *Clicks* are the number of times your ad was clicked.
- *Click-through rate (CTR)* is the total clicks divided by the total impressions.
- *Spend* is the total value spent on clicks.
- *Advertising cost of sales (ACoS)* is your total spend divided by your total sales as a percentage.
- *Return on ad spend (ROAS)* is your total sales divided by your total spend as a percentage.
- *% of orders new-to-brand* is the percentage of total orders that are new-to-brand orders.
- *% of sales new-to-brand* is the percentage of total sales (in the local currency) that are new-to-brand sales.

- *New-to-brand orders* are the number of first-time orders for products within the brand over a one-year look-back window.
- *New-to-brand sales* are the total sales (in the local currency) of new-to-brand orders.

Sales Attribution

One of the key things you'll want to know, as an advertiser, is how and when a sale is attributed to your campaign.

Sales are attributed only to the last campaign the user clicked (last-touch model), but also includes sales of products other than those in the campaign the consumer clicked on. Sales are also attributed for sales from other products within the inventory within 14 days for Vendor and 7 days for Seller.

You can see this from your "purchased product" report in Seller Central. Unfortunately, this report is not available via Vendor Central at the moment.

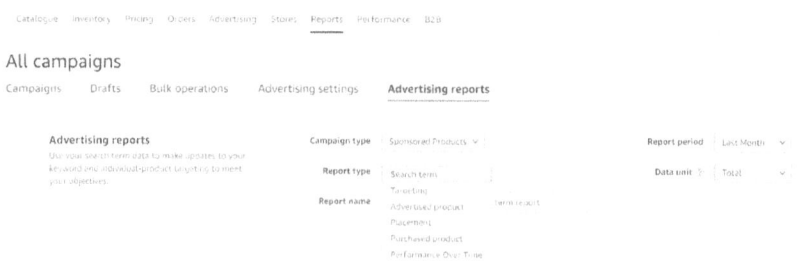

Sponsored Products Reports

The report below shows one ASIN being advertised and another ASIN being sold from the inventory of the same account. There is a halo effect of ads. Sales are attributed only to the last campaign the user clicked (last-touch model), but also includes sales of other products than those advertised.

Managing your Advertising Cost of Sale (ACoS)

ACoS is the main indicator to find out how efficiently your campaigns are running. If your ACoS goal is determined prior to the campaign, it helps to optimise your campaigns in the best possible way and remain profitable.

ACoS can be broken down to campaign, ad group or keyword level – if you want to be a bit more granular.

ACoS = ADVERTISING EXPENSES TOTAL ÷ TOTAL AD SALES X 100

Example: keyword "green baby bib"

For example, a seller makes £10 using the keyword "green baby bib"

Sales at the advertising cost of 0.50p, then the ACoS is 0.50 ÷ 10 x 100 = 5%. Here, per sale, it's costing 50p. So, we have invested 5% of the sales value for advertising.

$$\text{ACOS} = 0.50 \text{ ADVERTISING COSTS} \div £10.00 \text{ SALES X } 100 = 5\%$$

ACoS is positively correlated with the ad spend and negatively correlated with profit, i.e. if the ACoS increases, your ad spend increases and profit decreases.

How do I optimise my campaigns?

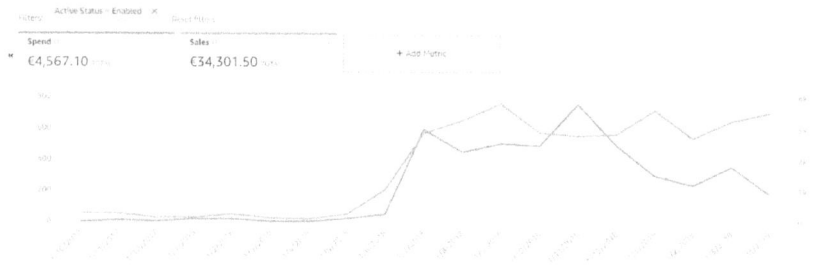

Spend vs Sales advertising report

The next step is to improve your campaign's returns which means increase sales and reduce ACoS.

1. Optimise your product content:

Review your product information, based on performance. If there's less conversion with high traffic, something's not right with the keywords or perhaps the price is not working for consumers. Review your search terms. Are you including very broad or non-related keywords? Make sure you're still winning the buy box. If you have a large number of products and are finding it difficult to keep track of prices, consider an automated repricer.

If you're a new seller with your brand, you will need at least three months, one feedback and one review to win the buy box. Alternatively, use FBA from the start.

2. Product categories:

Organise your product inventory by top sellers, brand or category. This helps you keep an eye on your products and quickly find the right products to identify for your Amazon PPC campaigns.

3. Campaign structure:

CAMPAIGN A	Product Type A	CAMPAIGN B	Product Type A
ADGROUP 1	Product Sub group	ADGROUP 1	Product Sub group
ADGROUP 2	Product Sub group		
ADGROUP 3	Product Sub group		

Notes
Keep similar products in 1 group
Keep product variations in 1 group
This ensures reporting is to the product level

Campaign Structure

Think about your campaign structure. Some find success with a granular structure with each product having its own ad group or campaign.

4. Keyword optimisation:

Keyword targeted campaigns require ongoing optimisation. When you start advertising with auto campaigns, you'll get a list of customer keywords that are generating traffic and sales.

Amazon takes your content as a source of keywords which is why having relevant content is vital.

It makes sense to add negative keywords that are not converting for a period of time.

Avoid adding negative keywords after running a campaign for a short time. If there are relevant keywords that are not convert-ing, allow a certain spend on each keyword. Some businesses don't negate relevant keywords until they spend £20.00 with no sales.

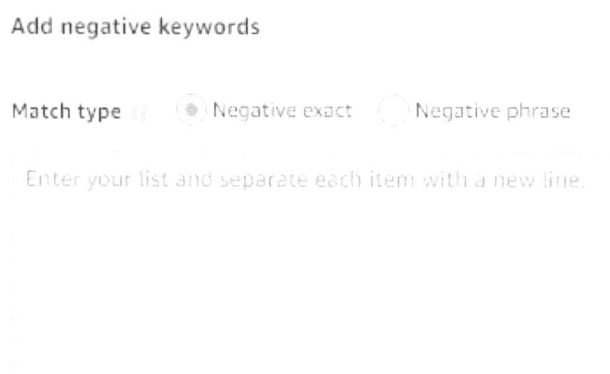

- Add Negative Phrase if you'd like to suppress your ad when there is a query with given keyword plus additional word before after that keyword

- Add Negative Exact if you you'd like to suppress your ads

5. Budget:

If your campaigns are working well within your target ACoS, it makes perfect sense to increase your budget. You can always start with small increases and continue until you see sales growth. This allows your campaigns to run throughout the day. The graph below shows increased sales as a result of increased budget, on selected campaigns, to €100 a day.

Campaign setup checklist

- Create an auto campaign to kick things off
- Create manual campaigns with three ad groups per keyword match type
- Analyse the search terms report to determine which keywords convert and which do not

- Add converting keywords from auto campaigns into a manual campaign. Use the best-performing ones as an exact match
- Add non-converting/irrelevant keywords as negative keywords with auto campaigns
- Add all manual ad keywords as negative for your auto campaigns so you are leveraging auto campaigns to generate new keywords.

Amazon advertising is progressive and in time you'll be using the best performing keywords on your campaigns. Then, consider profitability from each keyword and start adjusting bids or pausing keywords that are not profitable anymore.

TAKING YOUR CAMPAIGNS TO THE NEXT LEVEL

How do I optimise my keywords?

As we've already seen, keywords play a vital role in the effectiveness of your Amazon Advertising campaigns. Making sure you're targeting the right keywords with the right bid is one of the secrets to success on the Amazon platform.

1. Create a list from advertising report:

The search term report contains actual keyword data, with performance metrics such as CTR, conversion rate and sales. This is the primary source of your keyword data.

- Use this search term report to identify irrelevant keywords and add them as negatives.
- Increase bids for the most converting keywords so you get continuous sales.
- Increase bids for keywords with low numbers of

impressions. This would suggest the win rate is quite low and therefore the advertiser is only winning a placement quite low down/hardly ever seen.

- The report also gives you Advertising Cost of Sale (ACOS) and Return on Ad Spend (ROAS) which help you to determine the profitability of your campaigns.
- Sales are attributed to any purchase within seven days from a click in Seller Central and 14 days from click in Vendor Central

External keyword tools such as sonar can provide valuable ideas for more keywords. They, however, do not rely on search queries alone for your products. As a secondary source, they're extremely helpful in expanding the scope of your keyword list.

2. Analyse the performance of each keyword to assess its strength

Weak keywords: Keywords with high spend and low conversion are best kept as negative to improve advertising efficiency.

Cost-effective keywords: Get a list of low-cost keywords.

3. Allocate optimum bid

Allocate a higher budget for successful keywords in manual campaigns. A higher budget improves your bid's win rate, giving keywords a better chance to generate impressions and therefore clicks.

Allocate all match types for each keyword into three groups. Exact match is not always a good target and the broad one is not a bad one either. So, your campaign will look like below

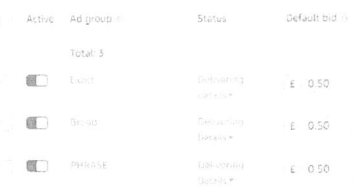

Campaigns with keyword match ad groups

Use negative keywords to limit the wastage. Use exact match type just so you don't stop additional traffic.

How do I optimise my ACoS?

The ACoS should always be less than the margin of your product after costs. If you have 43% margin after Amazon fees, manufacturing cost and shipping cost, then your ACoS must be less than this to stay profitable.

Total Sales	Amazon Fees	Shipping Cost	Manufacturing cost	Total Cost	Total Profit	Profit %
100	15	2	40	57	43	43

Amazon profit calculation

To lower your ACoS, your keywords must convert a higher amount of sales or you should reduce your spend.

. . .

1. Define target ACoS

Get your profit target for your sales on Amazon platforms. Once you have profit percentage, you can target your ACoS lower than this.

An example:

• You get a 43% profit before advertising and after all costs as seen above

• You need at least 20% on hand after advertising

• Your target ACoS should be 23% maximum

If the ACoS is higher than 23%, you are making a loss on every sale you generate via advertising. Although this is acceptable to get initial sales, in the long run, you should work towards lowering the ACoS.

2. Lower bids on high ACoS keywords

If your keywords are generating high ACoS, then reduce CPC bid.

3. Increase bids for high-performing keywords

For high performing keywords, it's best to increase bids just so your product appears most of the time when buyers use that keyword in their search. It's best to avoid any opportunity for lost sales.

· · ·

4. Add negative keywords

Any keywords that cost you more than they generate in sales, as seen in the screenshot below, should be added as negative keywords.

Keep in mind some keywords may take time to convert. So, have a plan to spend, say, £10.00 on keywords that are relevant, but not converting, before you stop.

Customer Search Term	Spend	7 Day Total Sale	Total Advertising Cost of
	€ 38 11	€ 44 99	84 7077%
h	€ 3 13	€ 20 00	15 6500%
a	€ 2 81	€ 20 00	14 0500%

The keyword with a very High ACoS and non-profitable

5. Pause variation ASINs that are non converting well

Pause any variation ASINs that are costing you with no sales, as seen in the screenshot below. Keep in mind that some ASINs may take time to convert, so, have a plan to spend say £10.00 before you pause.

Impressio	Clicks	▾ Spend	Orders	Sales
56,186	526	£121.63	5	£250.93
19,563	230	£57.74	2	£103.97
13,166	106	£25.60	2	£108.97
12,741	114	£21.19	1	£37.99
10,716	76	£19.10	-	-

The ASIN with no sales

6. Automated bid management support for Amazon PPC

There are quite a few external tools which help automatically adjust your bids. Automation takes care of your ACOS goals by adjusting bids automatically based on historical performance data of each keyword and their respective conversion rates.

How do I structure my campaigns for success?

The structure you give in your campaigns will affect how many ads you can display at one time as well as how easy it is for you to manage your keywords and gain insights into consumer behaviour.

Auto campaigns: You can structure this based on product types, category, top sellers or seasonal campaigns.

Here are some examples of campaign structure.

Manual campaigns: These are generally the second phase of advertising. By that time, you know what keywords are performing well and what is not. Spend a bit of time thinking about your structure. Check out some examples above. A very granular campaign would have one or a group of similar products, divided into three groups with BROAD, PHRASE and EXACT match. In this case, you have full control over each keyword.

Granular Manual campaign with three ad group with keywords match types

It's best to keep both auto and manual campaigns working hand in hand. Auto campaigns may initially create some additional cost, but, when negative keywords are added, the wastage can be lowered and you have the opportunity to increase the exposure of your products.

Automated and Manual Ads working together

With advertising, you spend a lot of time researching keywords and auto campaigns eliminate a lot of this work, allowing you to focus on other marketing activities. You'll know the best performing keywords from your search term report.

Organising your campaigns into portfolios

Advertising Portfolios make it easier to organise campaigns by product category or season and manage total spending with budget caps. If you're launching a range of products, it makes sense to assign a budget cap to those product campaigns, just so you don't over or underspend.

Amazon Advertising Portfolio

Portfolios are available with all sponsored ads and applicable at a campaign level. Some examples of how you could use Portfolios:

- Deals portfolio in which we up all the bids and use to increase awareness while a product is on a deal
- Brand awareness portfolio that focuses on generic keywords and predominantly SBs
- Competitor portfolio with the top five competitors per category and campaigns that use SPAs to target

each of them. You can get some really interesting insight which generates clicks and converts!

- Block and defend SPAs on your own products. These ads are there to mostly keep your product pages *clean* from competitors but also function as cross-selling and upsell opportunities

Sponsored Brand Ads (SBAs) and Sponsored Display Ads (SDAs)

As your business grows, you'll want to consider more of the options in the Amazon Advertising toolkit. As we've touched on above, SBs and SDAs both have a role to play in your marketing strategy. However these generally do not have as efficient ACoS as SPAs, which is why we suggest you start your advertising campaigns here!

GETTING STARTED WITH SBAS

Amazon Advertising screenshot

As a Seller Central user, you can access campaigns via Campaign Manager, the "Advertising" tab, including

"Manage Campaigns"> "Create Campaign". As a Vendor Central user, you will see SDA as an additional option.

Simply follow the below steps...

Step 1

Once you follow the SB link, you'll be asked for a campaign name, start date, end date, budget and your choice of products or store ad.

It's always best to name the campaign as clearly as you can, so anyone reviewing the campaign knows instantly what it's for. Avoid abbreviating, as that can cause confusion for someone who is not familiar with the campaign. The end date is optional, but it's important that you review the campaign periodically. Daily budget varies depending on how much budget you have available and what your goal is

Then, pick a landing page, either an Amazon Store or a product list with three or more products. While all three products don't necessarily have to have the same features, you should make sure that they're all relevant for the keywords you're selecting.

Some private label brands may have only two products, in which case, you should explore creating multi-buy or bundled product offerings.

Campaign name

Example: Christmas favourites

Portfolio

No Portfolio ⇕

Start   End

30 Jun 2019   No end date

Budget

£ 10.00   Daily ∨

Brand

FLEUR PARFUMERIE

Landing page for ad traffic

○ Amazon Store (including subpages)
Increase brand awareness and product discoverability by sending shoppers to your Amazon Store featuring a collection of your brand's products

● New product list page
Create a page featuring 3 or more of your products to be featured on a product list page.

Step 2

Choose a list of three products or more which share a common list of keywords. As your product ratings appear, with this campaign type, you should display products with 4-star ratings and above. As the placements are highly visible, it's the best practice to choose your best selling products.

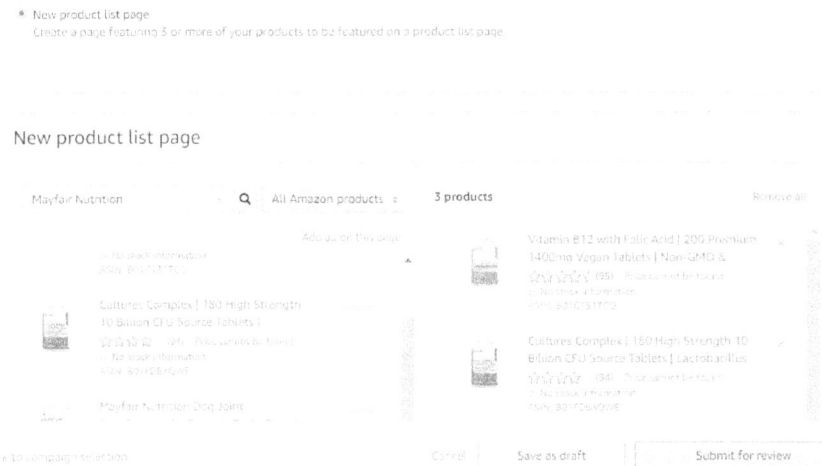

If you choose to drive traffic to an Amazon store, Amazon will suggest some products from your store. You have a few choices here, too. Start with advertising your home page and then progressively create Sponsored Brand Ads for your various subcategories.

If you have one or two products, create product-specific pages and use Amazon store target ads.

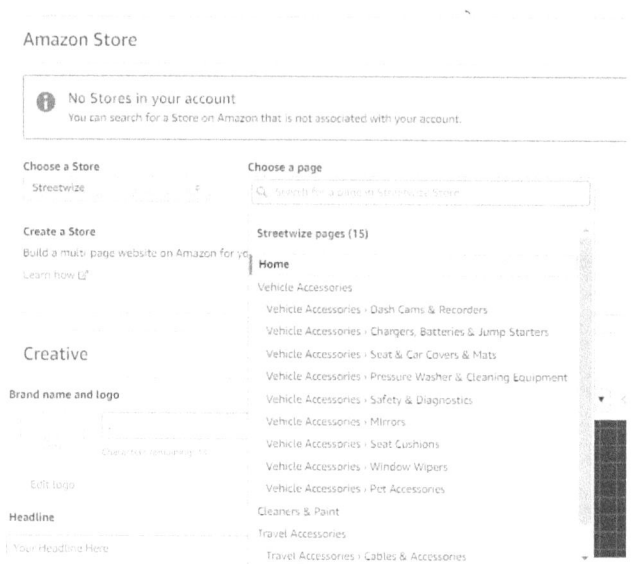

Step 3

This is the creative part. Include your brand name (maximum of 30 characters) and the headline that best describes your brand. You are limited to 50 characters. It makes sense to keep the headline in line with the keywords you've selected for the campaign.

Include your brand logo (at least 400 x 400px). If you have text within the image, make sure it's readable.

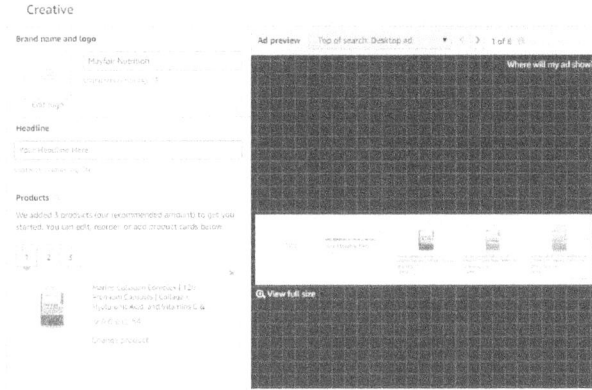

Step 4

In this step, choose three products for your ad. There is a preview screen so you can see how the final ad will look. You'll also see options to see preview ads across different platforms.

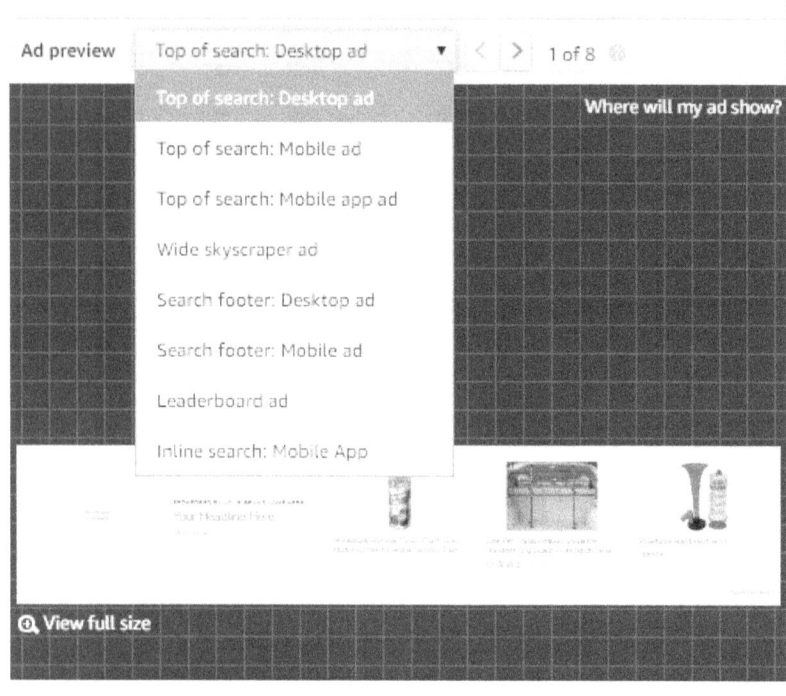

Step 5 - Targeting

Amazon offers keyword and product targeting options, as discussed before, but let's start with keyword targeting.

Add keywords with appropriate match types and bids. You'll notice a higher default bid of £0.95 or £1.50 to start with. While this isn't a minimum, you should expect winning bids will be higher than SPAs.

Automated bidding

☐ Allow Amazon to automatically optimise bids for placements below top of search.

✔ Set a custom bid adjustment

| Decrease by | 50 % | for placements below top of search |
| Increase by | | |

Automated bidding

☑ Allow Amazon to automatically optimise bids for placements below top of search.

With regards to auto optimisation, choose automated bidding so Amazon lowers your bids for fewer premium placements based on your conversion rate in that placement. This enables you to optimise toward conversion as much as possible.

If you're more focused on brand awareness, then turn off auto bidding. If you'd like to manually control your bidding, you can also do this here.

Add relevant keywords and their match type and also take some Amazon suggestions, if they're relevant to your advertising goal.

Set a custom bid adjustment

Increase by ∨   30   %   for placements below top of search

For example a 40% decrease on a £5.00 bid will become £3.00

Suggested	Enter keywords	Upload file

Suggested	Match type
roof	Broad
roof rack	Phrase
mats	Broad
battery charger	Phrase
car mats	Phrase
seat	Broad
trolley	Broad

Phrase and exact match keywords increase your chance of selling with an effective price. So, you can use the same keywords with different match types and allow Amazon to choose which to display.

NEW Broad match modifiers

For Sponsored Brands, you can now choose words that must be present in the shopper search in order for your ad to run.

Broad match modifiers can be added by adding the plus symbol "+" in front of the keyword. For example, if you use the keyword "milk +jugs" with a broad match, then the ad will only match to searches that contain the word "jugs". The ad may match to "churn jugs" or "jugs for gravy" but not to any search term that does not contain the word "jugs or jug."

Step 5 - Product Targeting

The product targeting option allows you to target categories or individual products just like you do with the SPAs.

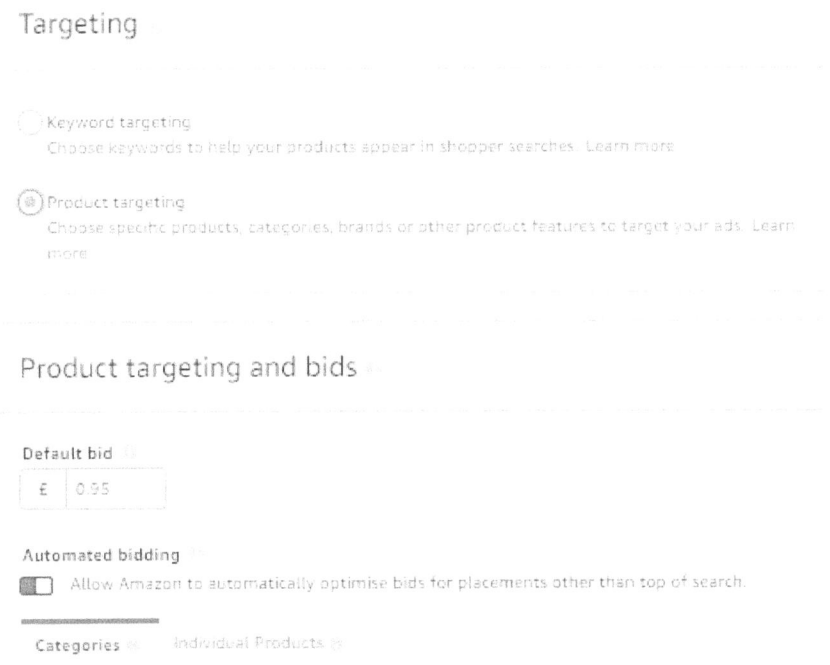

Choose single or multiple categories in a single campaign or separate campaigns.

Step 6

Amazon recently added negative keywords as an option for SBs, which you can use to add non-relevant keywords. For instance, if you sell bathroom scales, you may want to add kitchen as a negative keyword.

Step 7

You will notice Amazon displaying win rates for all keywords based on past searches. This is a very helpful metric displaying the percentage of the impression you can expect, based on the bids. The slide is there to compare win rate vs bids.

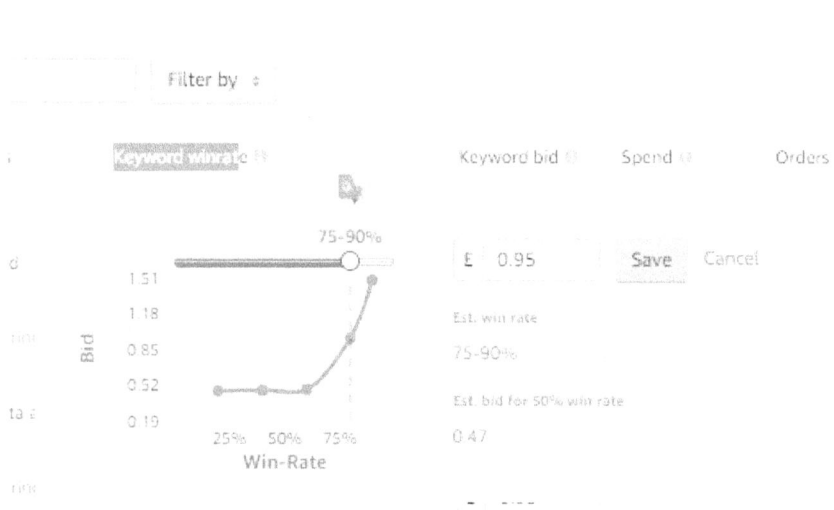

Step 8

Finally, review your campaign and "submit for review". It can take up to 72 hours for the review.

Key Metrics Explained

Most of the metrics have been explained with SPAs above. However, below are some key metrics a lot of brands follow because these metrics show the percentage of new customer wins.

New customer acquisition is normally expensive, although you may be willing to bear a higher ACoS for a new customer.

The new customers are based on their 12 months of purchase history.

- *% of orders new-to-brand* is the percentage of total orders that are new-to-brand orders.
- *% of sales new-to-brand* is the percentage of total sales (in the local currency) that are new-to-brand sales.
- *New-to-brand orders* are the number of first-time orders for products within the brand over a one-year look-back window.
- *New-to-brand sales* are the total sales (in the local currency) of new-to-brand orders.

You can improve your ACoS for SBs overall and manage what you're willing to spend on new customers by splitting campaigns and targeting branded and non-branded terms, allowing you to bid lower for your branded campaigns. You can do this by the following:

- Campaign A: Broad match "+[Your brand name]"
- Campaign B: Negatively target "[Your brand name]"

Managing your Advertising Cost of Sale (ACoS)

We have already talked about how ACoS is calculated. With SBs adjust bid and pause keywords based on your campaign goal.

GOALS	ACoS
Drive brand awareness / Competitive	Higher ACoS accepted
Drive Sales	Profitable ACoS accepted

Advertising Reports

There are four reports available for SBs.

Search term reports as seen below, show the performance of each target along with customer search terms like the SPA search term report. SPA category and product target display in the sponsored related products, but the result below shows this isn't the case with SB ads.

Targeting	Customer Search Term	Cost Per Click	14 Day Total	Total Advertising C
category="Cereal & Snack Bars"	quest bars	£ 0.36	£ 112.83	7.9677%
category="Cereal & Snack Bars"	quest bars	£ 0.39	£ 90.91	2.1450%
asin="b003v1wwhe"	quest	£ 0.13	£ 46.67	5.7853%
category="Cereal & Snack Bars"	quest choc chip	£ 0.42	£ 40.00	1.0500%
category="Cereal & Snack Bars"	high fibre cereal	£ 0.34	£ 29.92	1.1364%
asin="b007cx0zsk"	soy flour	£ 0.07	£ 24.78	1.1299%
asin="b002dyizh6"	albumen powder	£ 0.08	£ 24.16	1.7384%
category="Cereal & Snack Bars"	pulsin	£ 0.25	£ 24.00	26.1250%

Keyword placement reports show the performance for each keyword in the different position and SB can be displayed in. Most of the higher sales are from the top of the search results.

When analysed

- ACoS for the top of the search was 24% and
- ACoS for the other placements was 20% and
- 80% of the sales from SBAs were from the top of the search and
- 20% from other placements.

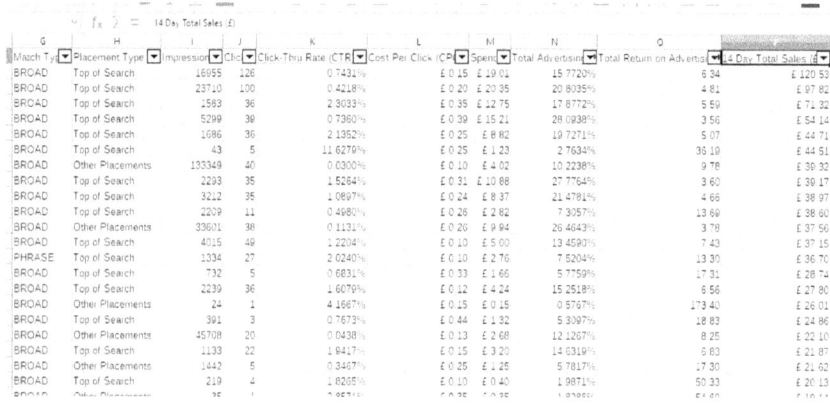

Match Type	Placement Type	Impressions	Clicks	Click-Thru Rate (CTR)	Cost Per Click (CPC)	Spend	Total Advertising	Total Return on Advertising	14 Day Total Sales (£)
BROAD	Top of Search	16955	126	0.7431%	£ 0.15	£ 19.01	15.7720%	6.34	£ 120.53
BROAD	Top of Search	23710	100	0.4218%	£ 0.20	£ 20.35	20.8035%	4.81	£ 97.82
BROAD	Top of Search	1563	36	2.3033%	£ 0.35	£ 12.75	17.8772%	5.59	£ 71.32
BROAD	Top of Search	5299	39	0.7360%	£ 0.39	£ 15.21	28.0938%	3.56	£ 54.14
BROAD	Top of Search	1686	36	2.1352%	£ 0.25	£ 8.82	19.7271%	5.07	£ 44.71
BROAD	Top of Search	43	5	11.6279%	£ 0.25	£ 1.23	2.7634%	36.19	£ 44.51
BROAD	Other Placements	133349	40	0.0300%	£ 0.10	£ 4.02	10.2238%	9.78	£ 39.32
BROAD	Top of Search	2293	35	1.5264%	£ 0.31	£ 10.88	27.7764%	3.60	£ 39.17
BROAD	Top of Search	3212	35	1.0897%	£ 0.24	£ 8.37	21.4781%	4.66	£ 38.97
BROAD	Top of Search	2209	11	0.4980%	£ 0.26	£ 2.82	7.3057%	13.69	£ 38.60
BROAD	Other Placements	33601	38	0.1131%	£ 0.26	£ 9.94	26.4643%	3.78	£ 37.56
BROAD	Top of Search	4015	49	1.2204%	£ 0.10	£ 5.00	13.4590%	7.43	£ 37.15
PHRASE	Top of Search	1334	27	2.0240%	£ 0.10	£ 2.76	7.5204%	13.30	£ 36.70
BROAD	Top of Search	732	5	0.6831%	£ 0.33	£ 1.66	5.7759%	17.31	£ 28.74
BROAD	Top of Search	2239	36	1.6079%	£ 0.12	£ 4.24	15.2518%	6.56	£ 27.80
BROAD	Other Placements	24	1	4.1667%	£ 0.15	£ 0.15	0.5767%	173.40	£ 26.01
BROAD	Top of Search	391	3	0.7673%	£ 0.44	£ 1.32	5.3097%	18.83	£ 24.86
BROAD	Other Placements	45708	20	0.0438%	£ 0.13	£ 2.68	12.1267%	8.25	£ 22.10
BROAD	Top of Search	1133	22	1.9417%	£ 0.15	£ 3.20	14.6319%	6.83	£ 21.87
BROAD	Other Placements	1442	5	0.3467%	£ 0.25	£ 1.25	5.7817%	17.30	£ 21.62
BROAD	Top of Search	219	4	1.8265%	£ 0.10	£ 0.40	1.9871%	50.33	£ 20.13

Use the campaign report to gain a better insight into the overall performance of each campaign. It's a good way to get a quick glance into which campaigns result in delivering your sales and ACoS targets.

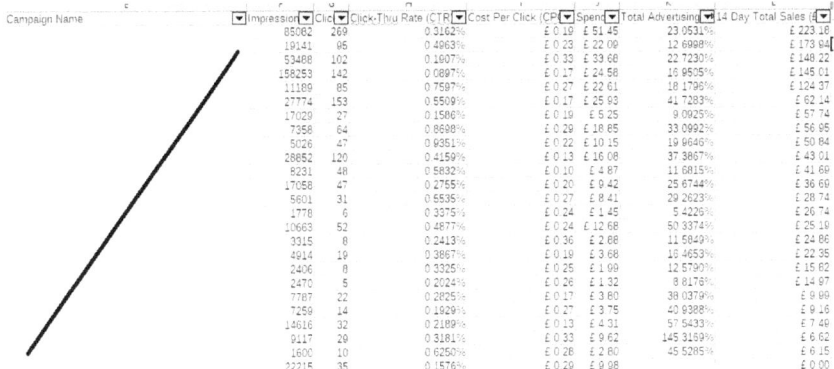

Campaign Name	Impression	Clicks	Click-Thru Rate (CTR)	Cost Per Click (CPC)	Spend	Total Advertising	14 Day Total Sales (£)
	85062	269	0.3162%	£ 0.19	£ 51.45	23.0531%	£ 223.16
	19141	95	0.4963%	£ 0.23	£ 22.09	12.6998%	£ 173.94
	53488	102	0.1907%	£ 0.33	£ 33.68	22.7230%	£ 148.22
	158253	142	0.0897%	£ 0.17	£ 24.58	16.9505%	£ 145.01
	11189	85	0.7597%	£ 0.27	£ 22.61	18.1796%	£ 124.37
	27774	153	0.5509%	£ 0.17	£ 25.93	41.7283%	£ 62.14
	17029	27	0.1586%	£ 0.19	£ 5.25	9.0925%	£ 57.74
	7358	64	0.8698%	£ 0.29	£ 18.85	33.0992%	£ 56.96
	5026	47	0.9351%	£ 0.22	£ 10.15	19.9646%	£ 50.84
	28852	120	0.4159%	£ 0.13	£ 16.08	37.3867%	£ 43.01
	8231	48	0.5832%	£ 0.10	£ 4.87	11.6815%	£ 41.69
	17058	47	0.2755%	£ 0.20	£ 9.42	25.6744%	£ 36.69
	5601	31	0.5535%	£ 0.27	£ 8.41	29.2623%	£ 28.74
	1778	6	0.3375%	£ 0.24	£ 1.45	5.4226%	£ 26.74
	10663	52	0.4877%	£ 0.24	£ 12.68	50.3374%	£ 25.19
	3315	8	0.2413%	£ 0.36	£ 2.88	11.5849%	£ 24.86
	4914	19	0.3867%	£ 0.19	£ 3.68	16.4653%	£ 22.35
	2406	8	0.3325%	£ 0.25	£ 1.99	12.5790%	£ 15.82
	2470	5	0.2024%	£ 0.26	£ 1.32	8.8176%	£ 14.97
	7787	22	0.2825%	£ 0.17	£ 3.80	38.0379%	£ 9.99
	7259	14	0.1929%	£ 0.27	£ 3.75	40.9388%	£ 9.16
	14616	32	0.2189%	£ 0.13	£ 4.31	57.5433%	£ 7.49
	9117	29	0.3181%	£ 0.33	£ 9.62	145.3169%	£ 6.62
	1600	10	0.6250%	£ 0.26	£ 2.60	45.5285%	£ 6.15
	22215	35	0.1576%	£ 0.29	£ 9.98		£ 0.00

Campaign placement report works in a similar way as the keywords placement report and you get an understanding of your campaign's overall performance based on placements. ACoS performance is identical to keywords placement report.

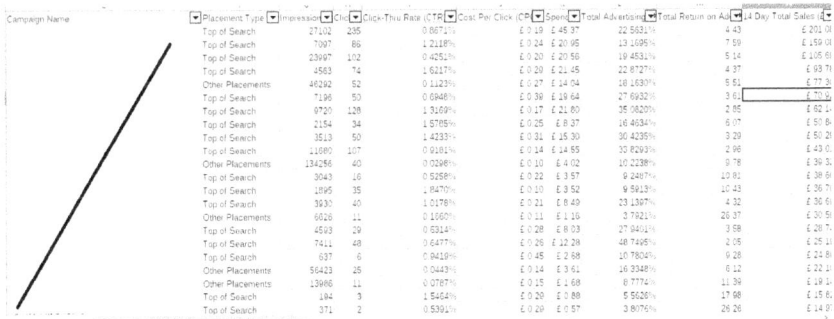

Campaign Name	Placements Type	Impression	Clicks	Click-Thru Rate (CTR)	Cost Per Click (CPC)	Spend	Total Advertising	Total Return on Ad	14 Day Total Sales (£)
	Top of Search	27102	235	0.867%	£ 0.19	£ 45.37	22.5631%	4.43	£ 201.06
	Top of Search	7097	86	1.2118%	£ 0.24	£ 20.95	13.1695%	7.59	£ 159.00
	Top of Search	23997	102	0.4252%	£ 0.20	£ 20.58	19.4531%	5.14	£ 105.69
	Top of Search	4583	74	1.6217%	£ 0.29	£ 21.45	22.8727%	4.37	£ 93.71
	Other Placements	46292	52	0.1123%	£ 0.27	£ 14.04	18.1630%	9.51	£ 77.31
	Top of Search	7196	50	0.6948%	£ 0.39	£ 19.64	27.6932%	3.61	£ 70.9
	Top of Search	9720	128	1.3169%	£ 0.17	£ 21.80	35.0820%	2.85	£ 62.1
	Top of Search	2154	34	1.5785%	£ 0.25	£ 8.37	16.4634%	6.07	£ 50.8
	Top of Search	3513	50	1.4233%	£ 0.31	£ 15.30	30.4235%	3.29	£ 50.2
	Top of Search	11880	107	0.9181%	£ 0.14	£ 14.85	33.8293%	2.96	£ 43.0
	Other Placements	134256	40	0.0298%	£ 0.10	£ 4.02	10.2238%	9.78	£ 39.3
	Top of Search	3043	16	0.5258%	£ 0.22	£ 3.57	9.2487%	10.81	£ 38.6
	Top of Search	1895	35	1.8470%	£ 0.10	£ 3.52	9.5813%	10.43	£ 36.7
	Top of Search	3930	40	1.0178%	£ 0.21	£ 8.49	23.1307%	4.32	£ 36.6
	Other Placements	6626	11	0.1660%	£ 0.11	£ 1.16	3.7921%	26.37	£ 30.5
	Top of Search	4593	29	0.6314%	£ 0.28	£ 8.03	27.9401%	3.58	£ 28.7
	Top of Search	7411	48	0.6477%	£ 0.26	£ 12.28	48.7495%	2.05	£ 25.1
	Top of Search	637	6	0.9419%	£ 0.45	£ 2.68	10.7804%	9.28	£ 24.8
	Other Placements	56423	25	0.0443%	£ 0.14	£ 3.61	16.3348%	6.12	£ 22.1
	Other Placements	13986	11	0.0787%	£ 0.15	£ 1.68	8.7774%	11.39	£ 19.1
	Top of Search	194	3	1.5464%	£ 0.29	£ 0.88	5.5026%	17.98	£ 15.6
	Top of Search	371	2	0.5391%	£ 0.29	£ 0.57	3.8076%	26.26	£ 14.0

We have analysed the same report to find out which placements help to bring new customers.

- 79% of the new to brand orders were from the top of the search and 20% from other placement
- Other placements brought 100 % of orders new-to-

brand orders where has only half of the orders from
the top of the search were NTB

	14 Day New-to-brand Sales (£)

F	G	H	I	J	K
Placement Type	Impressi	Clicks	Click-Thr	14 Day New-to-brand	14 Day % of Orders
Other Placements	46292	52	0.1123%	4	100.0000%
Other Placements	134256	40	0.0298%	4	100.0000%
Other Placements	6626	11	0.1660%	2	100.0000%
Other Placements	56423	25	0.0443%	2	100.0000%
Other Placements	13986	11	0.0787%	2	100.0000%
Other Placements	12044	9	0.0747%	2	100.0000%
Other Placements	1659	4	0.2411%	2	100.0000%
Other Placements	7419	16	0.2157%	1	100.0000%
Other Placements	3531	4	0.1133%	1	100.0000%
Other Placements	12071	7	0.0580%	1	100.0000%
Other Placements	3845	14	0.3641%	1	100.0000%
Other Placements	6336	13	0.2052%	1	100.0000%
Other Placements	2222	2	0.0900%	0	0.0000%
Other Placements	2684	6	0.2235%	0	
Other Placements	20183	8	0.0396%	0	

	14 Day New-to-brand Sales (£)

F	G	H	I	J	K
Placement Type	Impressi	Clicks	Click-Thr	14 Day New-to-brand	14 Day % of Orders
Top of Search	9720	128	1.3169%	8	100.0000%
Top of Search	7196	50	0.6948%	4	100.0000%
Top of Search	3043	16	0.5258%	4	100.0000%
Top of Search	1895	35	1.8470%	3	100.0000%
Top of Search	4593	29	0.6314%	3	100.0000%
Top of Search	119	2	1.6807%	2	100.0000%
Top of Search	1518	13	0.8564%	2	100.0000%
Top of Search	194	3	1.5464%	1	100.0000%
Top of Search	331	9	2.7190%	1	100.0000%
Top of Search	3513	50	1.4233%	7	87.5000%
Top of Search	3930	40	1.0178%	6	85.7143%
Top of Search	27102	235	0.8671%	19	82.6087%
Top of Search	7097	86	1.2118%	12	70.5882%
Top of Search	23997	102	0.4251%	7	70.0000%
Top of Search	4563	74	1.6217%	9	69.2308%
Top of Search	7411	48	0.6477%	2	66.6667%
Top of Search	11680	107	0.9161%	3	60.0000%
Top of Search	2154	34	1.5785%	3	50.0000%
Top of Search	637	6	0.9419%	1	50.0000%
Top of Search	371	2	0.5391%	1	50.0000%
Top of Search	1383	15	1.0846%	1	50.0000%
Top of Search	2032	27	1.3287%	0	
Top of Search	765	5	0.6536%	0	

SBs Campaign setup checklist

- Choose your goal: brand awareness or to drive sales
- Target an extensive list of keywords: brands, related product keywords and best performing keywords from your SPAs
- Utilise all match types: broad, phrase and exact
- Use Amazon's auction-based bids for better conversion rate
- Choose between a correct landing page
- A/B test your creatives including headline text, image and product choices
- Choose all match types to allow Amazon to use the best suitable option
- Choose appropriate win-rate based on your campaign goal

GETTING STARTED WITH SPONSORED DISPLAY ADS (SDAS)

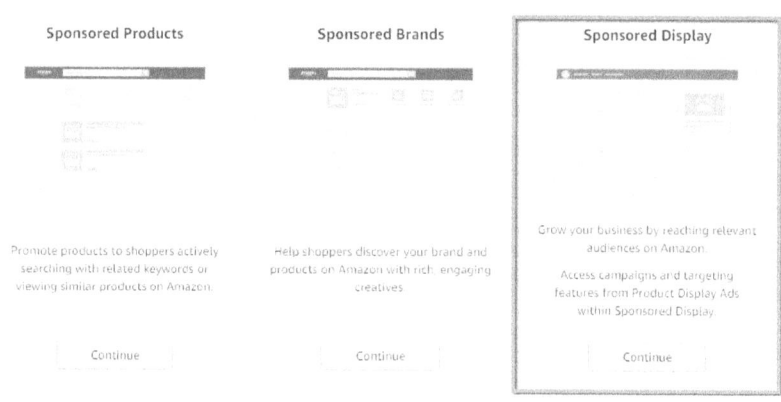

Amazon Advertising screenshot (Vendor Central UK View)

Access your ads via https://advertising.amazon.co.uk and simply follow the below steps.

Step 1 Choose "targeting" either product or interest-based

The initial step begins by choosing a method for "targeting". There are two options:

Targeting ⊛

◉ Audiences
   Choose which audiences you want to see your ads.

○ Product targeting
   Choose specific products or categories to target your ads.

- Audience targeting allows us to display to shoppers that are relevant to your products.
- Product targeting allows you to target particular ASINs or a particular category/categories.

Step 2 Choose a product to advertise

You have various targeting options in step 3, which is why you will see different options below.

Step 3 Start targeting based on your choice in step 1 (Option 1 Audience Vendor Central)

Targeting

Target by Audience

Target by Audience Interest

Step 3 Start targeting based on your choice in step 1 (Option 1 Audience Seller Central US)

Currently, SDAs are available to brands in the US Seller Central accounts with only placements across Amazon's third-party display network. Engagement is limited to shoppers who have previously viewed your products or products similar to yours, in the last 30 days, excluding shoppers who have purchased a similar product.

Step 3 Start targeting based on your choice in step 1 (Option 2 Product Targeting)

When you target by product Amazon allows you to target a specific product you'd like to appear against on their product pages.

Step 3 Start targeting based on your choice in step 1 (Option 3 Category Targeting)

Target by Categories

Target by Categories

Step 4 Update campaign settings including:

- Campaign Name: Assign an easy to understand name to help you analyse your campaigns later. This cannot be changed once set.
- CPC (Cost Per Click) Bid: Set appropriate bids per click here
- Budget: Allow daily budget or campaign budget including dates.

Step 5 Create ads, filling out all sections provided.

- Headline/Tagline: Use this limited 50 character space to creatively entice buyers to click on your ads. Use text like "Exclusive" or "New", "Buy Now" or "Save Now" and avoid any unsupported claims like "#1" or "Best Seller".
- Brand Name & Logo: Your brand name and logo are important to raise your brand awareness. Your logo must be 100 x 100 px.

Step 6 Preview your ads in seven different formats, including mobile. Review your choice of description and tagline so that your ad is visible in the best way possible across devices and formats.

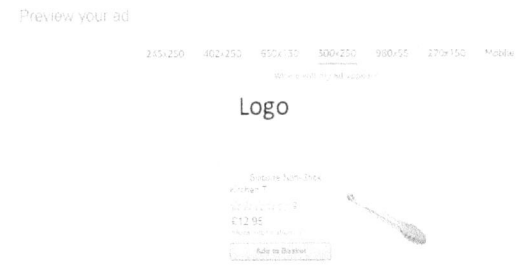

Step 7 Submit or save your campaign as a draft.

Your campaign will be submitted for review by Amazon.

Key Metrics and Reports

There isn't yet much detailed reporting for SDAs, so the key to the success of SDA is dependent on the products you target.

Audience targeting ads reporting shows which category of interest that is targeted but no details of conversion metrics for this. You will see the rest of the metrics like impressions, clicks, ACoS and sales.

Impressions	Clicks	Spend	Orders	▼ Sales	ACOS	Ac
1,535,140	623	£101.93	5	£57.55	177.11%	
57,598	12	£0.75	2	£40.89	1.84%	C

Category targeting ads report displays metrics against your selected category and you will see the success in each category target. Similarly, product target displays your listing of product targets but does not show metrics for each target.

As for the Amazon US Seller Central, we see conversion metrics based on two different targets: the first metric is for the shoppers who viewed our product and the second is for the shopper who viewed a similar product.

Active   Automatic targeting groups

Total: 2

Product views

Similar product views

Amazon does not tell us which product targets resulted in sales and this makes it difficult to analyse results. The report simply tells us the timestamp of sales.

SDAs Campaign setup checklist

- Choose your goal: audience vs product target vs category target
- Target a small batch of product, i.e. 10 to test
- Use phrases like buy now, exclusive or new
- Use Amazon's closely related product targeting to extend the reach
- A/B test your headline text
- Choose an appropriate bid rate based on Amazon's recommendation

Amazon Advertising Services

FOR VENDORS AND SELLER CENTRAL USERS

FIND OUT MORE

AMAZON ADVERTISING STRATEGIES

Competition is increasing as more advertisers flock in to take advantage of Amazon Advertising's high ROI. So, having a well-versed advertising strategy is critical to your success selling on Amazon.

Here are 3 Amazon advertising strategies that can apply to any Amazon sellers.

Market Penetration Strategy: This is an early stage of Amazon Advertising and the aim is to quickly penetrate your market and raise product awareness. You'd explore and learn with automatic ads, target relevant keyword then followed on by targeting competitive brand names and ASINs.

1 Amazon Advertising Strategy

	CAMPAIGN TYPE	TARGET
MARKET PENETRATION STRATEGY	SBAs – appears at the top of the search as a banner	Competitive terms – competitor brand names
	SBAs – appears at the top of the search as a banner	Generic Keywords
	SPAs – keywords targeted	Competitor brand names
	SPAs – asin targeted ads	Competitor ASIN's
	SPAs – keywords targeted	Generic Keywords
	SPAs – keywords targeted ads	Automatic Placement

Increase Market Share Strategy - At this second stage of advertising, our aim is to increase our market share and get sales which otherwise would not have been possible. Target categories to get placement on competing product pages and leverage display campaigns to enhance your brand awareness against competing products.

Amazon Advertising Strategy

	CAMPAIGN TYPE	TARGET
INCREASE MARKET SHARE STRATEGY	SPAs – category targeted ads	Sub-category
	SPAs – category targeted ads	Root-category
	SPAs – asin targeted ads	Related products which may not be exactly in the same category
	SDAs- asin targeted ads	Utilised SDAs to ensure we are appearing on competitor product pages, with the view of stealing their sale
	SBA - Cross Selling	We had several groups of products, supplied by client, which often sell together or are part of the same group. We set up SBA for each of these groups, including only these products, with the view that shoppers will add several of these products to their basket at once as they are related. This has been successful.

Defensive Strategy - At this 3rd stage of advertising, you'd defend product placement on Amazon pages and search results. You'd target your own brand name and target your own ASINs so by doing so there are fewer chances of other products appearing on your page.

Amazon Advertising Strategy

	CAMPAIGN TYPE	TARGET
DEFENSIVE STRATEGY	SBAs – appears at the top of the search as a banner, grabs shoppers attention	Brand terms – own brand names
	SPAs – normal keywords campaigns	Brands terms – own brand names
	SPAs – ASINS target	Own product ASIN's so customers will see our other products when they are on our page. Otherwise, they will see competitor product who may steal our sale.

USEFUL TOOLS

There is no other tool like your own search term report. It gives actual search queries from Amazon customers alongside metrics like clicks, impressions, CTRs. It is the primary source of keywords and acts as a valuable part of Amazon Search Advertising optimization.

There are some additional tools that can help you with the keyword research and if you are looking to automate your Amazon Search Advertising there are plenty of tools, too.

Tools	Features	Cost
Keyword dominator https://www.keywordtooldominator.com/	Gives you a list of Autocomplete keywords.	Free 3 searches per day
https://sellics.com	Amazon Advertising management tool	starts with $47
https://www.bidx-tool.com/en/	Amazon Advertising constantly optimizes your Ads.	starts with $89
https://intentwise.com/	Intentwise empowers Brands, Sellers and Agencies with precious insights, automation, and expertise.	$399
Sonar Tool http://sonar-tool.com/us/	The free tool provided by sellics. You can search by ASIN and keywords which displays relevant keywords directly on the Amazon page.	Free
https://datahawk.co/	Amazon analytics tools for sellers and vendors to increase sales, optimize margins, gain insights, and boost productivity.	$65
Keywordtool.io https://keywordtool.io/amazon	It is free to use a platform with a limited display of keywords. It has a good export function. This also gives search volumes and CPC information from Google ads and estimates CPC based on Google data.	$69
Google Keyword Planner	The Google Keyword Planner is also one of the best tools to find out keywords for your Amazon ads. Along with keywords, it allows you to enter the URL of a competitor and get a list of keywords relevant to their product.	Free

DAYTODAYEBAY

Are you looking to grow your Amazon business? Or would you like to get started selling on Amazon? We are specialist Amazon Consultants with over 10 years of experience, and our team of specialists can help you to grow your Amazon sales.

Daytodayebay is marketplace training and consultancy, for both Amazon and eBay. The company is led by Prabhat Shah who has 10+ years of marketplace experience.

We are one of very few UK Amazon agencies providing consultancy and training services in the UK and abroad. Our consultancy services come with no long-term contracts, and we can provide one-off content writing services and content optimisation. All of our training and consultancy can be tailored to your business.

With a team of Amazon experts with extensive experience working across different product categories in the UK and internationally, we provide services for both Vendor Central and Seller Central. We work flexibly at a reasonable cost.

Our Amazon Services include:

- Amazon Advertising Management

- Account Management
- SEO and Product Content Optimisation
- A+ and Amazon Store Design

Find out more and take look at case studies: https://www.daytodayebay.co.uk/amazon-services/